Mad Mega-Bad Day

Marg McAlister

Illustrated by
Margaret Power

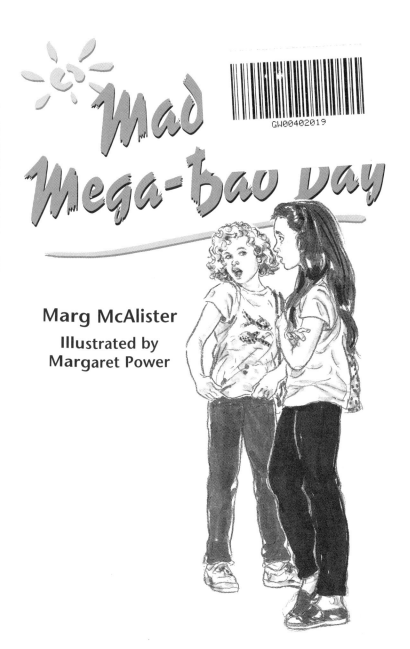

KINGSCOURT / McGRAW-HILL

Maddie's Mega-Bad Day
Copyright © 2002 Rigby Heinemann

Rigby is part of Harcourt Education, a division of
Reed International Books Australia Pty Ltd ABN 70 001 002 357.

Text by Marg McAlister
Map by Guy Holt

Illustrations by Margaret Power

Lettering by Georgia McKenzie, p. 3
Designed by Canary Graphic Design
Edited by Michelle Freeman

KINGSCOURT/McGRAW-HILL

Shoppenhangers Road, Maidenhead
Berkshire, SL6 2QL
Telephone: 01628 502730

Fax: 01628 635895

www.kingscourt.co.uk
E-mail: enquiries@kingscourt.co.uk

Printed in Australia by Advance Press

10 9 8 7 6 5 4 3 2 1

ISBN: 0-07-710337-8

Contents

CHAPTER 1

Sneaking Away!

MADDIE peered through the curtains, watching her brother Jake and his friend Leon get into the car across the road. Leon's big brother Rob was driving. They were off to the movies—without her.

Maddie gripped the curtain hard. She wanted to go, too. So what if they were meeting Leon and Rob's middle brother, Caleb, at the cinema. She didn't care about being the only girl. Why should they?

"How about I drive you to Dakota's place?" came her mother's voice from behind her.

"Dakota's not home," said Maddie crossly. "She's visiting her gran today."

"Is there anyone else you'd like to visit?"

1

"No. I want to go to the movies. Everyone's seen it except me!"

"Maddie, it's quite reasonable for Jake to go out with his friends," said her mother, in that trying-to-be-patient voice which Maddie hated. "I know you two are close, but you don't have to do *everything* together."

"I know that!" said Maddie. "But I *really* wanted to see that movie."

But there was no response from her mother, and a moment later, Maddie heard the screen door slide shut behind her. Her mother would be hanging out the washing.

Maddie tapped her finger against her chin, thinking. She had plenty of pocket money in her bedroom. Her mother had not forbidden her go to the movie—she had just said that Jake did not have to take her. She could catch a bus to town from just up the road. It wasn't any further than the bus to school.

2

That was what she would do—go on her own! She would sit by herself, then surprise the boys at the end of the movie and get a lift back with Leon's brother. Easy!

Pleased with her plan, she dashed into her room and changed into her new denim jeans and white, sparkly top. In her desk drawer she had nearly twenty-three dollars: plenty for the bus fare and a movie ticket. She grabbed a pen and paper and wrote:

Mum,
I've gone out for a while.
See you later.
Love Maddie

3

Maddie knew she would get into trouble for not saying where she was going or when she planned to be back—but she could deal with that later. Leaving the note on the kitchen table, she shouldered her tote bag, slipped out of the front door and ran down the road.

Perfect timing! When she reached the corner, she could see the bus coming, just two stops up the street. Panting, she waited for it to pull up at her corner, then climbed on.

"Big Oaks Shopping Centre, please," she said, handing over a five-dollar note.

"Sorry," said the bus driver. "You need a Number 32 bus to go there. I'm going to Marshfield Grove."

"Oh." Maddie felt stupid. "All right. Thanks."

Maddie hopped down again and watched as the bus rumbled off. She wished she had thought to ask the driver when a Number 32 bus would come along.

It was hot in the sun at the bus stop. After fifteen minutes, she was sweating. Her new jeans felt stiff and hot. Another bus came along, but it did not have the right number, either. A couple of stops along there was a bus stop with a shelter. A woman and a little boy about two years old were sitting there, enjoying the shade. Maddie decided to walk down and join them.

The woman smiled at her, then kept reading her magazine. The little boy had a lollipop in his mouth. He took it out and offered it to Maddie.

"Er ... no thanks," she said, looking distastefully at the saliva dripping from it.

"He just likes to share," said the woman. "Don't you, Jeremy?"

"That's nice," said Maddie, edging a bit further away from him.

Jeremy poked the lollipop at her again. He said something that sounded like "Bite?"

5

Maddie shook her head.

Jeremy frowned. "Bite!" he said loudly, and pushed the lollipop at her mouth. He let go. The lollipop rolled down the front of her new top and plopped in her lap.

"Yuck!" Maddie hastily picked it up by the stick, but it was too late. She had sticky bright green stains on her new white top. She looked at the mess in disgust. How could she turn up to the movies looking like this?

"*Naughty* Jeremy!" His mother picked
him up and sat him on her other side.
"I'm really sorry. He just likes to share
with people." She fished in her bag and
handed Maddie a crumpled tissue.
"Here—this might get some of it off."

"Want 'olliop! Want 'olliop!" howled
Jeremy, climbing over his mother's lap.

Maddie thrust his lollipop back at
him and scrubbed at the stains on her
top. But it did not help at all. In fact, she
made things worse. Now, she had bright
green stains with little bits of shredded
tissue stuck to them.

She could not go home to change, or her mother would demand to know where she was going. But to turn up at the movies like this! Should she just give up and go home?

The decision was made for her by the rumbling approach of the bus—this time, with a big "32" showing above the windscreen. Thank goodness! This would have to be it. She could try to get the stains out in a washbasin at the shopping centre.

Maddie climbed on board, making sure she stayed well away from generous Jeremy and his sticky lollipop. At least she was on the right bus. She should still be in time for the movie—as long as nothing else went wrong ...

CHAPTER 2

Lollipop Woes

MADDIE stepped down off the bus at the side entrance to the shopping centre and checked her watch. Good: only one-thirty. The movie didn't start until two-fifteen. Plenty of time! She headed straight for the women's restroom to scrub off the lollipop stains.

But it was not easy to clean her top. In fact, Maddie concluded gloomily as she rubbed at the stains with some crumpled paper towels, she had made them worse. Now they were a paler green, but had spread out more. And there were big damp patches all around them. Her new white top was soaked.

9

She sighed, pressed the button on the hot-air hand dryer, and stood close under it to dry her top.

"Hi, Maddie," said a voice behind her. "I thought it was you I saw coming in here. What are you doing?"

Maddie jumped guiltily and turned around. It was Dani, her new neighbour from across the road. She and Maddie had only spoken half-a-dozen times, and thrown a few hoops with Leon and Jake. Dani was smiling in a shy way, looking curiously at Maddie's top stretched out under the dryer.

"Hi," Maddie said. She glanced down at the big green splotches on her white top. "I got in the way of a kid with a lollipop. Just when I was about to go to a movie, too. Now look at me, I'm sticky *and* dirty." She stepped back away from the hand dryer and then shrugged. "Oh well, I suppose nobody will see it in the dark."

"Who are you here with?" Dani looked around, as if expecting some of Maddie's friends to pop up out of nowhere.

"No one. Jake's gone with his friends, so I came by myself." Maddie picked up her tote bag and heaved it on to one shoulder. She hesitated, then said, "Unless ... do you want to come?"

Dani looked tempted. "I'd have to ask Mum. She and Bianca are in a fashion store over there." She jerked her head towards the door. "Which movie?"

"*Millennium Starship*," said Maddie. "I'll come with you while you ask your mum."

11

Dani's mum and Bianca were just coming out of the store opposite. "Hey, Dani, we were looking for you," said Bianca.

Bianca turned and smiled at Maddie. "They have some terrific bargains in there. There's a table of T-shirts for only five dollars each—and they look great!" She pulled one out of a bag and held it up.

"Only five dollars?" said Maddie. She quickly glanced down at her splotchy top. She had enough money to buy a new T-shirt *and* see the movie. Then she would not have to feel embarrassed by the stains. "I might go in and get one, and change before I go to the movie."

"And I'd like to go to the movie, too," Dani said quickly to her mother. "Is that okay?"

"Who's with you, Maddie?" asked Dani's mother. "How will you get home?"

"I'm here on my own," said Maddie. "I caught the Number 32 bus."

"Oh." For a moment, Dani's mother looked undecided. "On your own? Hmmm … I'm just about to take Bianca to visit her friend Marisa—we won't be home until about six. If Dani goes, she'll have to wait at your place after the movie, Maddie. Would that be okay with your mother?"

Maddie nodded.

"Well, as long as you know which bus to catch … all right. Make sure the two of you stay together, don't talk to strangers, and come straight home after the movie." Dani's mother took out twenty dollars. "Dani, buy yourself a couple of new T-shirts—you need them badly. And use the change for the movie and the bus home. You've got some money for snacks, haven't you?"

"Yes. Thanks, Mum!" Dani smiled.

Maddie could hardly believe her luck. From being on her own at home she was about go to a movie with a new friend. Better and better!

She and Dani waved goodbye to Bianca and Dani's mother, and then pushed their way through the crowds into the store.

"I don't think my mother would have let me come on the bus by myself," said Dani. "You're lucky."

"Well…" Maddie hesitated. "Mum doesn't actually know. I just left a note to say I was going out."

"You *what?*" Dani stared at her. "Does that mean when we get home you're going to get into trouble?"

"Probably," said Maddie. "Oh well, I'm here now."

14

Maddie edged her way towards the T-shirt table. "Mum might not be quite as mad if you're with me."

Fifteen minutes later, they were both at the counter paying for their T-shirts. Maddie ducked across to the restrooms and changed into her new top, stuffing the stained one into her bag. Within ten minutes, they were lining up for movie tickets.

That was when Maddie discovered that her purse was missing.

CHAPTER 3

What Else Can Go Wrong?

"DANI!" she gasped, scrabbling furiously in her bag. "My purse! It's gone!" She started pulling things out of her tote bag and gave them to Dani to hold. The stained T-shirt. Her phone card in its plastic wallet. Her address book. Three pens. A pack of tissues. A torn-out magazine article she was saving for a friend. An empty crisp packet. Finally, she reached the bottom of her bag. No purse.

Dani tugged her out of the line. "I saw you with it when you paid for your T-shirt. Did you leave it on the counter in the store?"

Maddie shook her head tearfully. "No. I remember walking away and putting my change into my purse." She thought hard. "It must have fallen out of my bag when I changed my top. It's probably still on the floor in the cubicle!"

The two of them ran back to the restroom. Maddie searched everywhere. No purse.

"It's gone!" she moaned. "First, my new top gets ruined, then I lose my purse. I should have just stayed at home."

Dani checked her own purse. "I've got enough to get us both into the movies, but then we can't pay for a bus home. And Mum can't come and get us."

The two girls looked at each other. Maddie bit her lip. What a choice. Go to the movies and not have enough money to get home—or catch the bus home without seeing the movie. She certainly did not want to phone her mother and tell her she was stuck at the shopping centre. Then she would be really mad.

"I know," Maddie said. "We can get a lift back with Jake and his friends. They came with Leon's brother. He can take us, too!"

Dani looked happier. "Are you sure they'll do it?"

Maddie nodded confidently. "They wouldn't just leave us here. And they came to see this movie—so we just have to race out at the end and wait until they come through the doors. Easy! We can't miss them."

"Well … I really would like to see this movie …" Dani looked back at the ticket office.

Everything had gone wrong that could go wrong, Maddie decided. She was going to be in trouble anyway. After she had gone to all this bother to see the movie, she was not about to give up and go home now! "We're late already," she said. "Come on!"

19

An hour-and-a-half later, she and Dani hurried for the doors as soon as the movie finished. They stood there watching everyone file out, talking about the movie. All too soon it was obvious that Jake and Leon weren't there. Finally, the usher walked out and closed the doors.

Maddie and Dani looked at each other. "I thought you said they were coming to this movie?"

"They *were*," said Maddie. "They've been looking forward to *Millennium Starship* all week. They wouldn't change their minds now. So—where are they? Why aren't they here?"

"And," said Dani, "how do we get home?"

Maddie sighed. "I'm going to have to phone Mum, I suppose. But let's walk around for a bit first. See if we can see them—" Suddenly, she stopped. "Wait a minute. They might be at the *other* cinema. The old one outside the shopping centre."

Dani shrugged. "I'm new around here."

"Let's go and see!" Almost running, Maddie led the way out of the shopping centre.

The old cinema—she had forgotten all about that. It often ran movies at a special price to win people away from the modern cinema.

The two of them raced down the street. They hadn't even reached the theatre when Maddie pointed. "There they are!" she shouted.

"Where?" Dani looked around.

"See? That's Leon, in the bright red T-shirt." Maddie increased speed. "Jake! Leon! Rob!"

At last the boys heard her and turned around. Jake looked surprised.

"What are you doing here?" he asked when Maddie came puffing up to him. "Did Mum bring you?"

21

"No. I caught a bus." Maddie didn't want to say too much more in front of his friends. "Dani and I went to see the movie over at the shopping centre."

"You caught a bus?" Jake frowned. He knew Maddie wouldn't be allowed to catch a bus to town on her own. "Oh— with Dani."

Maddie let him assume they had come in together. "But I lost my purse, and Dani had to pay for me to go to the movie—and now we don't have enough for the bus fare home. Can we go home with you?"

"With us?" Jake shook his head. "There are four of us plus Rob driving—Caleb and his friend Brad met us here. There's no room in the car."

Maddie gave a huge sigh. Nothing, absolutely *nothing*, was going right today. Well, except for meeting Dani.

"But do you have enough money for our bus fares?" she asked hopefully.

"Sorry." Jake looked at the others. "Anyone else?"

A chorus of "no" sounded. Even twenty-year-old Robert shrugged. "Sorry, Mads. I'm flat broke after today. Spent my last twenty dollars on fuel for the car on the way here."

"Bad luck. Looks like you're going to have to phone Mum. Rather you than me!" Jake grinned. "See you later!"

The boys went off, making "Oooh–er! You're in trouble!" noises.

Gloomily, Maddie watched them walk off down the street and around the corner to the car park. Then she took out her phone card.

"Oh well," she said. "Might as well get it over with." She walked over to the phone booth at the entrance of the old cinema, lifted the receiver, then slipped the card into the slot.

CHAPTER 4

Stuck in Town

NO LUCK.

Slowly, Maddie moved the phone away from her ear. She glanced at Dani and shrugged. "You wouldn't believe it. The phone card has run out."

Dani looked in the direction the boys had gone. "If we run, we might be able to catch the boys. They can tell your mum that we need a lift."

"No." Maddie was still mad at Jake. If he had let her come in the first place, she wouldn't be in this fix! "We'll just find a coin phone and ring." Then she remembered that she had lost her purse. "That is... if you've got enough change for a phone call?"

Dani counted her money. "Let's see … twenty cents … thirty … yep, sixty cents. Plenty!"

They trudged back to the shopping centre. Maddie wondered what Dani was thinking. They had had a good time at the movie—but now, because of Maddie, they had no way to get home. Maddie grimaced. It was usually Jake who rushed into things and got into trouble, not her. She was the "practical" twin—the organiser. But she had not organised this very well!

"Sorry about all of this, Dani," she said, as they went back in through the shopping centre entrance.

"That's okay," said Dani. "It was a good movie." She pointed to a wall of phones. "Over there. Here's the money."

Maddie dropped the coins in the slot and punched in her home number. It was busy. "Just my luck," she said. "I hope Mum's not on the Internet. She'll be there for hours."

Dani looked curious. "What? In chat rooms?"

"No, she designs websites. If no one else is home, she usually stays online. Dad's been telling her to get another phone line." Maddie tried the number again. "Nope. Still busy." She leaned back against the phone booth. "Now what?"

"If she's online, you could send her an email," suggested Dani. "There must be an Internet cafe here somewhere."

"One problem," said Maddie. "Sixty cents isn't enough to log on."

"Oh." Dani looked worried for a moment, then laughed. "This is turning out to be one of those days when nothing goes right. Don't worry. We'll be fine."

Maddie raised her eyebrows. "We might not get through to Mum until dark," she pointed out. "Then she'll be freaking out and we'll *really* be in trouble. Well, I will be, anyway."

"No, everything's going to be all right," Dani assured her. "We should just start walking."

"I'm not hitch-hiking," Maddie warned her. "You never know—"

"Of *course* not hitch-hiking," said Dani. "Just walking. Someone we know will come along. Let's go."

Maddie trailed after her, frowning. The way Dani talked you would think she had a personal line to the future. Dani was new to the area—who did she expect to see driving past? It would take at least an hour-and-a-half to walk home. Maddie *really* didn't feel like a ninety-minute hike.

They walked out of the shopping centre and started down the main road. The sun was still hot on their backs, even though it was past four o'clock. Finally, Maddie asked, "What makes you so sure someone's going to come along?"

"I just know." Dani seemed to hesitate, then make up her mind to speak. "I have these hunches about things. I know if things are going to work out or not."

Maddie was intrigued. "What, all the time? You mean you know whether you'll pass a test—stuff like that?"

"Well, no, not like that exactly. It's not like I can see into the future. But sometimes I can tell that there's danger ahead. Or if things look bad, I might know that it's all going to turn out okay."

29

"Like someone coming along to give us a lift home?" Maddie looked around. "Can't see anyone yet."

Dani smiled. "Give it time. We only left the shops five minutes ago."

Maddie was fascinated. "Does it work all the time? Say a thunderstorm was brewing and a bolt of lightning was going to strike us. Would you know?"

"I might. Yes, probably."

Maddie thought about it. "How? I bet you'd see the clouds, or feel the electricity in the air. That's how you'd know." She hitched her bag onto the other shoulder. "I mean, you didn't know ahead of time that I was going to lose my purse, did you? Or is that not the same thing?"

"No, it's not," said Dani. "Mum says my hunches are more like an animal's instinct. Sort of intuition."

Maddie's curiosity grew. "Tell me about a time when you knew there was danger coming. What happened?"

Dani said nothing. After a moment's silence, Maddie turned her head to look at her. Dani's face had a strange expression—sad and angry all at the same time. Seeming to know that Maddie was looking at her, she turned her face away, bent to pick up a stick and rattled it against the fence of the house they were passing.

Rattle. Rattle. Rattle. "Another time, maybe," she said finally.

Oakfield
Park

HAZEL ST

MULBERRY V

rst Gordon
ptist Church

CHID RD

SYCAMORE

DA

St.
Pres
Ch

N HWY

Maddie gave her a sideways look. What could it be that would make Dani look like this? All tight and forbidding. She just *had* to know.

"Go on, tell me now," she pleaded. "Just give me one example."

Dani threw the stick away. Then she stopped walking. Maddie stopped, too, and looked at her.

"If I tell you, then you have to promise not to tell anyone else," Dani said.

"Okay," said Maddie, surprised. What could be such a big secret?

"No, you have to promise," said Dani. "Say it."

"All right, I promise."

CHAPTER 5

Secrets and Promises

DANI'S brown eyes seemed almost to be looking right through Maddie. As though she was looking at something else entirely. Maddie suddenly realised she was remembering something. But what?

"The last time I knew there was danger around," said Dani, "was when my sister was in an accident." At last she looked away from Maddie. "Dad was driving. He was in a really bad temper, and I wouldn't get into the car because I knew something bad was going to happen. That made him even madder. He drove away really fast with Bianca beside him, and didn't brake in time at the traffic lights and skidded into another car. And Bianca lost her leg and hurt her spine so she's in a wheelchair."

The last sentence came out in a rush, and Dani looked at Maddie challengingly. "But you can't tell anybody!"

"All right, I won't," said Maddie. She was stunned. Dani's *father* was the reason Bianca was in a wheelchair? It was going to be hard to keep this from Jake. She and Jake did not keep secrets from each other. "But I can tell Jake, can't I?"

"You promised you wouldn't tell!" Dani looked panicky. "If you tell Jake, he'll tell Leon, and Leon'll tell someone else, and then the whole school will know!"

34

"Okay, okay," Maddie soothed her. "It's just that I tell Jake everything, because we're twins. But I won't if you don't want me to." She hesitated. "What happened to your dad?"

"He got charged by the police and he has to go to this driver education program. And now dad has to go to meetings about controlling his temper, too." Dani started walking faster. She was tall, and her long legs made it difficult for Maddie to keep up easily. "I don't know if he'll come back to live with us again." *This explains Dani's behaviour*, Maddie thought. She had not been able to figure Dani out; one minute she was friendly, the next she seemed distant. Now, Maddie understood. Dani was worried people would find out what her father had done.

35

Dani, still walking fast, suddenly stopped in front of an old house with an overgrown garden. Maddie nearly ran into her. "What?"

"Ssshhh, listen," said Dani, holding up a hand.

They both listened, looking around them. The street was deserted, apart from the occasional car going past. Then Maddie heard it too—a faint cry from behind a mass of tangled shrubs in the front garden of the old house.

They moved closer to the fence and peered through the shrubs. All Maddie could see was more greenery. "Hello?" she called. "Is anyone there?"

"Help!" came a muffled voice. "*Help!*"

Maddie ran to the gate. It was old and flecked with rust. It squealed painfully when Maddie pushed it open. She had to squeeze through a tiny space to get through.

"Come on, Dani."

Dani crammed herself into the space after Maddie, and they pushed their way through the overgrown garden.

"I'm here," called the voice, a little louder now. "Over here!"

Maddie abruptly found herself in a tiny clearing of grass in front of an even tinier verandah. She felt Dani looking over her shoulder.

In front of them was a dog's kennel. Quite a large dog's kennel, but with a small doorway. Sticking out of the opening to the kennel was the back of a flowery dress and a pair of freckled legs in brown sandals.

"Um, are you okay?" said Maddie, which she immediately thought was a stupid thing to say, seeing as the woman had been calling for help.

"No," came the faint voice. "I'm stuck! Can you help me out?"

Maddie and Dani tried not to laugh. How did she manage to get in there?

It must be horrible to be stuck in a smelly dog's kennel on a hot day.

"Sure," said Maddie. She tentatively approached the legs. "Do you want us to pull?"

"No," said the voice. "My shoulders are stuck inside. You'll have to take the kennel apart."

Take the kennel apart? They studied the doghouse. It looked pretty solid.

"Have you got a hammer?" asked Maddie.

"In the shed around the back," said the woman's voice. "You'll find other tools there, too."

"I'll go," said Dani. She rushed around the side of the house and disappeared.

Maddie prodded at the wood of the kennel. Yes, solid all right. Then she examined the roof. It was made of sheets of tin. They might come off fairly easily. At least then the woman would be able to breathe fresh air.

38

She looked around. There was an overgrown rock garden to the left of the house. Perhaps she could bash the roof off with a big rock? She walked over and heaved at one of them. It was buried too deep. She chose a smaller one, and with a grunt she hauled it out of the ground.

"What are you doing?" asked the voice faintly.

"Getting a rock," said Maddie. "I'm going to try to knock the roof off so you can breathe."

"Oh. Okay. Don't cut yourself," said the voice. One of the feet sticking out of the kennel wriggled a bit.

Maddie held the rock in both hands and swung it, hitting a sheet of tin under the lip of the roof. The kennel rocked, but the roof stayed on. She swung the rock again. The same thing happened. "This doesn't seem to be working too well," Maddie told the woman. "I'll try it one more time."

39

She smashed the rock against the roof again, and this time the edge of the roof bent upwards with a screech. A nail popped out.

"Here, let me try," said Dani's voice behind her.

Maddie stepped out of the way. Dani had found a hammer and a crowbar. She inserted the crowbar in the gap Maddie had made, and both girls leaned down on it.

The roof screeched up another few centimetres. In a few minutes, they had the roof ripped up on one side.

A very red-faced woman turned her head and peered up at them. Sweat was dripping down her face. "Thank goodness," she said. "I'm lucky you two came along."

"Wow," said Maddie. "You really are stuck." The woman's arms were both inside the doghouse. One hand was gripping a new-looking doll. The other arm was bent underneath her. It looked extremely uncomfortable.

"My pup ran away with the doll and hid it in the kennel," the woman said. "When I tried to get it out ..." She sighed. "Well, you can see what happened. Can you knock out the front of the kennel?"

"Yep," said Dani confidently. "Hang on." She inserted the crowbar into a join. "Ready?"

"Ready," said the woman. She screwed her eyes up tight.

CHAPTER 6

The Rescue

"HERE we go," said Dani. She tapped the crowbar firmly into place with the hammer, then they both leaned on the bar again. There was a groan as the wood moved. The girls rocked back and forth, putting all their weight on the bar. At last, a piece of wood came free, and Maddie smashed at it with the hammer.

Suddenly, the front of the kennel came away. It split into two pieces, falling either side of the woman.

With a loud groan, she wriggled backwards. Out came her legs. Out came her arms. And, finally, out came her hand, still gripping the doll. The woman sat up creakily.

"Ouch!" she rubbed her side. "Oh, thank goodness! And thank *you!*"

Looking a bit wobbly, she stood up. Her face was the colour of a tomato. "So much for Ernie's kennel," she said, looking at the wreckage.

"Is Ernie your husband?" asked Maddie. She supposed he would not be too happy about his lovely kennel being a heap of smashed wood.

"No, Ernie's the dog. Well, it serves him right for stealing my doll." She gave them a wavery smile. "Come inside and wash your hands. I'll give you a drink."

"Thanks, but we'll have to go," said Maddie, looking at her watch. The rescue had taken them twenty minutes. "We've still got a long way to go to get home."

"Just have a quick drink first," said the woman. "It's the least I can do."

Dani shrugged. They both followed the woman inside. There were dolls everywhere. Dolls in modern clothes, dolls

44

in rags, dolls in full ruffled dresses, dolls with ringlets and dolls with braids, dolls with long hair and dolls with short hair.

"Wow," said Maddie, gazing around in awe. "I've never seen so many dolls in my life."

"It's my business," said the woman. "I'm Vera Connelly, by the way. I win prizes with these dolls. That's why I had to get this one back from Ernie—she's my latest project. Believe me, it would cost you a lot of money to buy this."

The girls introduced themselves in return. Then they washed the dirt and sweat off their hands and had a drink of lemonade. "You know," said Dani, still staring around her, "I've never liked dolls much, but these are beautiful— and really different."

Vera smiled. "That's why I win prizes," she said. "And since you like them so much, I'll give you one each as a reward for rescuing me!"

45

"No need," said Maddie, feeling uncomfortable. "You said they're worth a lot of money. It's okay."

"I want to," said Vera. "You can see I've got plenty. Choose one each."

"What, *any* doll?" said Dani.

"Any doll."

Dani pointed to a doll with short spiky hair and a cheeky expression. "Could I have that one?"

"Good choice. That one won first prize five years ago." Vera fetched it for her. "What about you, Maddie?" she asked.

Maddie felt a bit embarrassed. She had never really been a "doll" person. But there was something about a doll at the back that appealed to her. This one had dark red hair piled up in ringlets, and was holding a mask on a stick to its face. The dress was made of brilliant greens and blues and sat out in plump layers. "Um—that one?"

"It's yours."

Vera left the room for a moment and came back with two big carrier bags. "Here. This way they'll stay in good condition while you get home."

"Thanks," they chorused.

"We really have to go," Maddie said. "Mum will be wondering where we are." She looked at her watch again. It was well after four-thirty—and home was more than an hour's walk away.

Trouble ahead!

With Vera thanking them all the way to the gate, they hurried away.

47

Dani's Hunches

"**Well**, there's one thing about going out with you, Maddie," said Dani. "You can't say it's boring." She was walking fast, with long strides that left Maddie puffing trying to keep up.

"Thanks. I think," gasped Maddie. "Hey, can you slow down?"

"I thought you were in a rush to get home?"

"I am, but not *that* big a rush." She threw Dani a sideways glance. "Anyway, according to you, someone we know will come along, right?"

Dani nodded. "Probably. But even if that's not what happens, it'll be okay. You'll see."

Maddie wished she could feel that sure. She didn't quite believe in Dani's "hunches" yet. She thought again about what Dani had told her. About Dani not wanting to get into the car before the accident, and about Bianca's injuries. Maddie wanted to ask more questions, but somehow knew it wouldn't be a good idea. She could ask later—when she knew Dani better.

They walked for another ten minutes, then turned into the main road that wound downhill for about eight blocks before their street. Maddie's legs were getting really tired.

That was when Dani's "hunch" proved to be correct. Driving towards them came Robert's car. He drove past, did a U-turn and pulled up alongside them. Leon and Jake grinned at them from the passenger seats.

Leon wound down his window. "Want a lift?"

49

Maddie looked at Dani. "I don't believe this. How did you *know* they would come along?"

Dani shrugged. "I told you. I have hunches." She climbed into the back seat beside Jake, then Maddie got in.

"What are you doing here?" said Maddie.

"I got home," said Jake, "and Mum asked if I knew where you were. She was getting worried."

"I knew she would be," said Maddie. "Oh boy, I'm for it. What did you say?"

"I said I thought you were with Dani." He grinned. "Well, it's the truth, isn't it? I'll leave it to you to tell her where you went. I bet she didn't say you could go to the movies, did she?"

50

"Don't *you* start giving me lectures," said Maddie. "Thanks for not telling on me, though. How did you know where to find us?"

He pointed at Leon. "His idea. He thought you might have started walking."

Leon looked around from the front seat. "Same story as always," he said. "The Raven twins get into trouble, and Leon comes to the rescue."

"Or Leon's brother," said Rob from the driver's seat. "I always seem to get the job of bailing you kids out." He looked at Leon. "Especially my little brother. Mum and Dad think you're just perfect—but Caleb and I know different!"

"I *am* perfect," said Leon with his super-charmer grin.

"Oh *yeah*," said Maddie. "All the adults think so, but we know what you're really like. You can just fool them better than we can."

Maddie grinned at Leon. She had heard her mother comment on "what a charmer" Leon was. Somehow when the rest of them got into trouble, Leon always managed to escape. His friends and brothers were always joking about it. "Thanks for coming to get us, Rob."

"No worries," he said. "Just do me a favour and tell your mum where you're going next time, okay?"

52

Maddie and Jake wrinkled their noses at each other. Leon's brother was nice, but sometimes he lectured them just like their parents. "Okay," said Maddie.

Rob turned into Sunrise Avenue, and then into his driveway next to Dani's house. "Okay," he said. "I've done my bit. Now you can explain where you've been. Good luck!"

Maddie sighed. *Here we go!* she thought.

CHAPTER 8

A Day to Remember!

MADDIE walked across the road and into her house, with Dani following. Her mother emerged from her office, scowling. "Maddie! About time. Where have you *been* all day? I turn my back to hang out some washing, and you disappear— leaving a note that tells me nothing!" She looked at Dani, and stopped frowning. "Hi, Dani. How are you?"

"Fine, thanks, Mrs Raven." Dani looked at the floor.

"I don't mind you going to visit Dani, Maddie," her mother explained, "but you should have told me where you were."

Maddie stood silently for a moment. She *could* let her mother think that she had just been across at Dani's all afternoon.

But if she found out they had been to the movies, Maddie would be in even more trouble for not telling the truth. She would have to confess.

"Well, actually, Mum," she started, "you'll never guess—"

She was interrupted by her mother's gasp. "What have you got there?"

"Huh?" Maddie didn't know what she meant for a moment, then followed her mother's gaze to the huge plastic carrier bags she and Dani were holding. "Oh, the dolls," said Maddie. She had forgotten all about them while trying to think of how to get out of trouble. "That's a part of it. You wouldn't *believe* what happened to us today."

Her mother's eyes narrowed. "Uh-oh," she said. "I already don't like the sound of this. Every time you or Jake start a sentence with '*You wouldn't believe*...' I know I'm not going to like what's coming."

"It's nearly always Jake," said Maddie, miffed, "not me."

"Well, it's you today," said her mother. "Better start explaining, young lady."

Maddie really hated it when her mother called her "young lady". It always meant a lecture. But one look at her mother's face told her that she had better tell the truth. Somehow her mother always knew if she was leaving bits out, too. It was really annoying!

So Maddie started right at the beginning. She told her mother about Jeremy and the lollipop, about meeting Dani, and about losing her purse, finishing with rescuing Vera from the doghouse and being given the dolls as a reward.

Her mother's mouth dropped open. "She gave you these dolls for rescuing her from the *doghouse?*"

"Yes." Maddie nodded hard. "She really did." She pointed to the phone number on the carrier bags. "You can phone her and ask!"

"Do you have any idea what Vera Connelly's dolls *cost?*" asked her mother.

"She told us that they cost a lot of money." Maddie was amazed her mother had even heard about the doll-maker. "Why? Is she famous?"

"She's been in the local paper heaps of times," said her mother. "I can't believe you rescued her! And she *gave* you these dolls." She shook her head. "It's not just that they cost a lot of money—they're so well made that they're collector's items. No wonder she was trying to save the one that the pup took away. Anyway…"

Then Maddie's mother got that firm look in her eye. "Anyway, you're still in big trouble. It sounds like it's lucky for Vera that you came along, but you were doing the wrong thing. You *know* you're not supposed to go to town by yourself."

"Well, it's no further than catching the bus to school—" Maddie started, then stopped as she caught sight of her mother's serious expression. "Okay. I know. I'm sorry."

Maddie had to put up with a few minutes of the "stranger danger" lecture and the "why your parents need to know where you are" lecture, with Dani squirming in embarrassment alongside. As she realised how worried her mother had been, Maddie felt hot and cold all over, and promised herself that she would think things through a little more—next time.

But in the end, it seemed her mother wasn't too angry. She actually asked Maddie to tell the doghouse rescue story all over again. "Vera Connelly, *imagine!*" she kept saying.

Finally, she let them go. "Just one more thing, Maddie," she called, as the girls headed off towards Maddie's room.

Maddie looked back. "Yes?"

"Next time," said her mother, "do the right thing and you won't end up in the doghouse yourself, okay?" Then she laughed as though she had just told the funniest joke in history.

Maddie rolled her eyes. "Sure, Mum." She grabbed her new friend Dani by the arm. "Come on. Let's get out of here."

All in all—it had not been such a bad day after all!